Cal

by Iain Gray

Lang Syne

PUBLISHING

WRITING *to* REMEMBER

LangSyne
PUBLISHING
WRITING *to* REMEMBER

E-mail: info@lang-syne.co.uk

Distributed in the Republic of Ireland by Portfolio Group,
Kilbarrack Ind. Est. Kilbarrack, Dublin 5.
T:00353(01) 839 4918 F:00353(01) 839 5826
sales@portfoliogroup.ie
www.portfoliogroup.ie

Design by Dorothy Meikle   Printed by Martins the Printers

© Lang Syne Publishers Ltd 2011

ISBN 978-1-85217-297-8

Callaghan

MOTTO:
Faithful and bold.

CREST:
An arm with the hand
holding a sword
entwined with a snake.

NAME variations include:
Ó Ceallacain *(Gaelic)*
O'Callahan
O'Gallaghan
Callahan
Callaghane
Ceallachan
Cellachain
Ceallachain
McCallaghne

To Niamh

lots of love

from Daddy. x

Chapter one:
Origins of Irish surnames

According to an old saying, there are two types of Irish – those who actually are Irish and those who wish they were.

This sentiment is only one example of the allure that the high romance and drama of the proud nation's history holds for thousands of people scattered across the world today.

It's a sad fact, however, that the vast majority of Irish surnames are found far beyond Irish shores, rather than on the Emerald Isle itself.

The population stood at around eight million souls in 1841, but today it stands at fewer than six million.

This is mainly a tragic consequence of the potato famine, also known as the Great Hunger, which devastated Ireland between 1845 and 1849.

The Irish peasantry had become almost wholly reliant for basic sustenance on the potato, first introduced from the Americas in the seventeenth century.

When the crop was hit by a blight, at least 800,000 people starved to death while an estimated two million others were forced to seek a new life far from their native shores – particularly in America, Canada, and Australia.

The effects of the potato blight continued until about 1851, by which time a firm pattern of emigration had become established.

Ireland's loss, however, was to the gain of the countries in which the immigrants settled, contributing enormously, as their descendants do today, to the well being of the nations in which their forefathers settled.

But those who were forced through dire circumstance to establish a new life in foreign parts never forgot their roots, or the proud heritage and traditions of the land that gave them birth.

Nor do their descendants.

It is a heritage that is inextricably bound up in the colourful variety of Irish names themselves – and the origin and history of these names forms an integral part of the vibrant drama that is the nation's history, one of both glorious fortune and tragic misfortune.

This history is well documented, and one of the most important and fascinating of the earliest sources are *The Annals of the Four Masters*, compiled between 1632 and 1636 by four friars at the Franciscan Monastery in County Donegal.

Compiled from earlier sources, and purporting to go back to the Biblical Deluge, much of the material takes in the mythological origins and history of Ireland and the Irish.

This includes tales of successive waves of invaders and settlers such as the Fomorians, the Partholonians, the Nemedians, the Fir Bolgs, the Tuatha De Danann, and the Laigain.

Of particular interest are the *Milesian Genealogies*,

because the majority of Irish clans today claim a descent from either Heremon, Ir, or Heber – three of the sons of Milesius, a king of what is now modern day Spain.

These sons invaded Ireland in the second millennium B.C, apparently in fulfilment of a mysterious prophecy received by their father.

This Milesian lineage is said to have ruled Ireland for nearly 3,000 years, until the island came under the sway of England's King Henry II in 1171 following what is known as the Cambro-Norman invasion.

This is an important date not only in Irish history in general, but for the effect the invasion subsequently had for Irish surnames.

'Cambro' comes from the Welsh, and 'Cambro-Norman' describes those Welsh knights of Norman origin who invaded Ireland.

But they were invaders who stayed, inter-marrying with the native Irish population and founding their own proud dynasties that bore Cambro-Norman names such as Archer, Barbour, Brannagh, Fitzgerald, Fitzgibbon, Fleming, Joyce, Plunkett, and Walsh – to name only a few.

These 'Cambro-Norman' surnames that still flourish throughout the world today form one of the three main categories in which Irish names can be placed – those of Gaelic-Irish, Cambro-Norman, and Anglo-Irish.

Previous to the Cambro-Norman invasion of the twelfth century, and throughout the earlier invasions and settlement of those wild bands of sea rovers known as the Vikings in the eighth and ninth centuries, the population of the island was relatively small, and it was normal for a person to be identified through the use of only a forename.

But as population gradually increased and there were many more people with the same forename, surnames were adopted to distinguish one person, or one community, from another.

Individuals identified themselves with their own particular tribe, or 'tuath', and this tribe – that also became known as a clann, or clan – took its name from some distinguished ancestor who had founded the clan.

The Gaelic-Irish form of the name Kelly, for example, is Ó Ceallaigh, or O'Kelly, indicating descent from an original 'Ceallaigh', with the 'O' denoting 'grandson of.' The name was later anglicised to Kelly.

The prefix 'Mac' or 'Mc', meanwhile, as with the clans of the Scottish Highlands, denotes 'son of.'

Although the Irish clans had much in common with their Scottish counterparts, one important difference lies in what are known as 'septs', or branches, of the clan.

Septs of Scottish clans were groups who often bore an entirely different name from the clan name but were under the clan's protection.

In Ireland, septs were groups that shared the same name and who could be found scattered throughout the four provinces of Ulster, Leinster, Munster, and Connacht.

The 'golden age' of the Gaelic-Irish clans, infused as their veins were with the blood of Celts, pre-dates the Viking invasions of the eighth and ninth centuries and the Norman invasion of the twelfth century, and the sacred heart of the country was the Hill of Tara, near the River Boyne, in County Meath.

Known in Gaelic as 'Teamhar na Rí', or Hill of Kings, it was the royal seat of the 'Ard Rí Éireann', or High King of Ireland, to whom the petty kings, or chieftains, from the island's provinces were ultimately subordinate.

It was on the Hill of Tara, beside a stone pillar known as the Irish 'Lia Fáil', or Stone of Destiny, that the High Kings were inaugurated and, according to legend, this stone would emit a piercing screech that could be heard all over Ireland when touched by the hand of the rightful king.

The Hill of Tara is today one of the island's main tourist attractions.

Opposition to English rule over Ireland, established in the wake of the Cambro-Norman invasion, broke out frequently and the harsh solution adopted by the powerful forces of the Crown was to forcibly evict the native Irish from their lands.

These lands were then granted to Protestant colonists, or 'planters', from Britain.

Many of these colonists, ironically, came from Scotland and were the descendants of the original 'Scotti', or 'Scots', who gave their name to Scotland after migrating there in the fifth century A.D., from the north of Ireland.

Colonisation entailed harsh penal laws being imposed on the majority of the native Irish population, stripping them practically of all of their rights.

The Crown's main bastion in Ireland was Dublin and its environs, known as the Pale, and it was the dispossessed peasantry who lived outside this Pale, desperately striving to eke out a meagre living.

It was this that gave rise to the modern-day expression of someone or something being 'beyond the pale'.

Attempts were made to stamp out all aspects of the ancient Gaelic-Irish culture, to the extent that even to bear a Gaelic-Irish name was to invite discrimination.

This is why many Gaelic-Irish names were anglicised with, for example, and noted above, Ó Ceallaigh, or O'Kelly, being anglicised to Kelly.

Succeeding centuries have seen strong revivals of Gaelic-Irish consciousness, however, and this has led to many families reverting back to the original form of their name, while the language itself is frequently found on the fluent tongues of an estimated 90,000 to 145,000 of the island's population.

Ireland's turbulent history of religious and political strife is one that lasted well into the twentieth century, a landmark century that saw the partition of the island into the twenty-six counties of the independent Republic of

Ireland, or Eire, and the six counties of Northern Ireland, or Ulster.

Dublin, originally founded by Vikings, is now a vibrant and truly cosmopolitan city while the proud city of Belfast is one of the jewels in the crown of Ulster.

It was Saint Patrick who first brought the light of Christianity to Ireland in the fifth century A.D.

Interpretations of this Christian message have varied over the centuries, often leading to bitter sectarian conflict – but the many intricately sculpted Celtic Crosses found all over the island are symbolic of a unity that crosses the sectarian divide.

It is an image that fuses the 'old gods' of the Celts with Christianity.

All the signs from the early years of this new millennium indicate that sectarian strife may soon become a thing of the past – with the Irish and their many kinsfolk across the world, be they Protestant or Catholic, finding common purpose in the rich tapestry of their shared heritage.

Chapter two:
Warrior kings

**The virile blood of ancient Irish kings courses proudly
through the veins of the thousands of Callaghans
scattered throughout the world today.**

It was from the celebrated Ceallachan, a tenth century
king of the south-western province of Munster that the
family takes it name – with 'ceallach' indicating 'strife', or
'war', although some other sources suggest it may stem
from 'bright-headed', or 'frequenter of churches.'

'War' or 'strife', however, would appear to be a more apt
meaning considering the warlike role the Callaghans played
for centuries on the stage of the drama that is Ireland's
history.

Inaugurated king of Munster in 936A.D., Ceallachan
forged a reputation as a fierce and determined warrior and,
in one of the many battles for control of the province,
defeated the father of the great warrior king Brian Bóruma
mac Cénnetig.

Better known to posterity as Brian Boru, it was this High
King who gave his name to the distinguished clan of
O'Brien, and who is famed for the defeat he inflicted on the
Vikings at the battle of Clontarf, north of Dublin, in 1014.

Ceallachan also gained distinction in his many battles
against the Vikings.

Mainly of Norwegian origin, it was in the closing years of the eighth century A.D. that their sinister longboats first appeared off Irish shores, and the monastery of St. Patrick's Island, near Skerries in present day Co. Dublin, was looted and burned to the ground.

Raids continued along the coastline until they made their first forays inland in 836 A.D., while a year later a fleet of 60 Viking vessels sailed into the River Boyne.

An indication of the terror they brought can be found in one contemporary account of their depredations and desecrations.

It lamented how 'the pagans desecrated the sanctuaries of God, and poured out the blood of saints upon the altar, laid waste the house of our hope, trampled on the bodies of saints in the temple of God, like dung in the street.'

By 841 A.D. the Vikings, or Ostmen as they were also known, had established a number of strongholds on the island, but their raids began to ease off before returning with a terrifying and bloody vengeance in about 914A.D.

They met with a determined resistance from the native Irish, most notably in the form of the forces of the powerful confederation of clans known as the southern Uí Neill, of which Ceallachan was a member.

He was of the Clan Eoghan, which took its name from a son of the legendary Niall of the Nine Hostage, progenitor of the O'Neills.

The Irish suffered a resounding defeat at the battle of Dublin in 919A.D., and it was not until just over thirty years later that the raids gradually came to an end.

But by this time the Vikings had established permanent settlements in Ireland, particularly in Dublin and other coastal areas such as present day Waterford, Wexford, Carlingford, and Strangford – indeed the names of the latter four stem from the Old Norse language of the Scandinavians.

But it was Ceallachan, from his stronghold at Cashel, in Co. Tipperary, who was responsible for driving the Vikings out of Munster.

The ancient Irish annals resound with his daring exploits.

The Saga of Ceallachan relates how, at the battle of Limerick, thought to have been fought between 934 and 941, the bold warrior put an army of Vikings to flight after the tide of battle had turned temporarily in their favour:

'... *when Ceallachan perceived that the soldiers were being slain... and that Clan Eoghan were being slaughtered, there arose his wrath, his rage, his vigour, and he makes a royal rush, caused by mighty fits of passion, at the nobles of the Lochlannachs [Vikings], while the noble race of Eoghan protect him.*

'*Ceallachan reached the warlike Amlaib and made an attack on the rough mail coat of the warrior, so that he loosened his helmet under his neck and split his head with hard strokes, so that the Lochlannach fell by him.'*

Claiming he wanted to end the hostilities, the Viking chieftain Sitric offered Ceallachan his daughter's hand in marriage and, despite being warned by Sitric's wife – who appears to have had something of a crush on the daring and handsome Munster king – that this was a trick, he travelled to meet Sitric to discuss terms.

The warning proved accurate as Ceallachan and a son of one of his Kennedy kinsmen were ambushed and captured.

Kennedy's father immediately assembled a vast army of the southern Uí Neill to seek retribution and, on learning of this, Sitric and his army boarded ships at Dundalk, north of Dublin, and tied Ceallachan to the mast of his own vessel.

But the massed forces of the southern Uí Neill were also skilled seamen and one of their number rammed the Viking vessel carrying Ceallachan.

With two swords in hand he jumped aboard and freed him and the pair managed to escape.

The Viking fleet was put to flight – one source relating how they were sent racing back to Norway – while Sitric was drowned.

The Viking threat to Munster had been quashed and Ceallachan subsequently consolidated his hold on the province.

He died 'a laudable death', according to the annals, in about 964A.D., with one source claiming that, perhaps fittingly, the fiery warrior was killed after being struck by lightning.

Muchadg ua Ceallachan, a grandson of the warrior, became the first to adopt the 'Ceallachan', or 'Callaghan' name, while Muchadg's grandson Carthach became the progenitor of the McCarthys.

The Callaghans and the McCarthys engaged in bitter feuds for control of territory, with the McCarthys eventually emerging triumphant and becoming the overlords of the Callaghans in the early years of the twelfth century.

Through time the Callaghans fulfilled the important function of acting as hereditary physicians to the McCarthys.

In the latter decades of the twelfth century both families, along with other native Irish clans, faced a common enemy in the form of invaders from across the sea.

These were not the Vikings of previous centuries, but brutal and ambitious Norman lords and their retainers who settled on the island in the wake of an invasion in 1169 – one of the most pivotal moments in Ireland's long history, and one that would change the Gaelic-Irish way of life forever.

Chapter three:

Oppression and revolt

Late twelfth century Ireland was far from being a unified nation, divided as it was into territories controlled by squabbling chieftains who ruled imperiously as kings in their own right.

In a series of bloody conflicts one chieftain, or king, would occasionally gain the upper hand over his rivals, and by 1156 the most powerful was Muirchertach MacLochlainn, king of the O'Neills.

He was opposed by the equally powerful Rory O'Connor, king of the province of Connacht, but he increased his power and influence by allying himself with Dermot MacMurrough, king of Leinster.

MacLochlainn and MacMurrough were aware that the main key to the kingdom of Ireland was the thriving trading port of Dublin, and their combined forces eventually took it.

But when MacLochlainn died the Dubliners rose up in revolt and overthrew the unpopular MacMurrough.

A triumphant Rory O'Connor entered Dublin and was later inaugurated as Ard Rí, but MacMurrough appealed for help from England's Henry II in unseating him.

The English monarch agreed to help him, but distanced himself from direct action by delegating his Norman subjects in Wales with the task.

These ambitious and battle-hardened barons and knights had first settled in Wales following the Norman Conquest of England in 1066 and, with an eye on rich booty, plunder, and lands, were only too eager to obey their sovereign's wishes and provide MacMurrough with aid.

MacMurrough managed to rally Cambro-Norman barons such as Robert Fitzstephen and Maurice Fitzgerald to his cause, along with Gilbert de Clare, Earl of Pembroke, also known as Strongbow.

They invaded Ireland in 1169, and their onslaught on the forces of O'Connor and his allies was so disciplined that by 1171 they had re-captured Dublin, ostensibly in the name of MacMurrough, and other strategically important territories.

Henry II now began to take cold feet over the venture, rightly fearing that he may have helped to create a powerful rival in the form of a separate Norman kingdom in Ireland.

Accordingly, he landed on the island at the head of an army in October of 1171 with the aim of curbing the power of his barons.

But protracted war was averted when the barons submitted to the royal will, promising homage and allegiance in return for holding the territories they had conquered in the king's name.

The king also received the reluctant submission and homage of many of the Irish chieftains, tired as they were with internecine warfare and also perhaps realising that as long as they were rivals and not united they were no match for the powerful forces the English Crown could muster.

English dominion over Ireland was ratified through the Treaty of Windsor of 1175, under which Rory O'Connor, for example, was allowed to rule territory unoccupied by the Normans in the role of a vassal of the king.

As the English Crown gradually consolidated its hold on the island, and with Anglo-Norman adventurers arriving to take advantage of the rich pickings available, many native Irish clans were dispossessed of their ancient territories.

The Callaghans were among the many victims, and by 1300 they had settled in present day Co. Cork after being pushed off their Co. Tipperary territories.

The area in which they settled was about five miles west of what is now the thriving town of Mallow – previously known as Pobal Uí Cheallachain, or 'O'Callaghan's Country', and situated on the banks of the Blackwater River.

It was a precarious existence – having to regularly battle with the increasing encroachment of Anglo-Norman adventurers into their territory while also occasionally battling with their neighbours – a trait they shared with their fellow Celts in the Highlands and Islands of Scotland.

Donnacha O'Callaghan, chief of the clan from 1537 until 1578, became infamous for his skills as a cattle raider – carrying out no less than 200 raids throughout Munster.

But the end was in sight for the Gaelic-Irish way of life of proud clans such as the Callaghans – a totally separate sept of which had been settled for centuries in the present day counties of Armagh and Monaghan in the province of Ulster.

This sept, it is believed, may originally have been known as Kealahan, or O'Kelaghan.

An indication of the harsh treatment meted out to the native Irish ever since the twelfth century invasion can be found in a desperate plea that was sent to Pope John XII by Roderick O'Carroll of Ely, Donald O'Neil of Ulster, and a number of other Irish chieftains as early as 1318.

They stated: 'As it very constantly happens, whenever an Englishman, by perfidy or craft, kills an Irishman, however noble, or however innocent, be he clergy or layman, there is no penalty or correction enforced against the person who may be guilty of such wicked murder.

'But rather the more eminent the person killed and the higher rank which he holds among his own people, so much more is the murderer honoured and rewarded by the English, and not merely by the people at large, but also by the religious and bishops of the English race.'

The plight of the native Irish deteriorated further through the English Crown's policy of settling, or 'planting' loyal Protestants on Irish land.

This policy had started during the reign from 1491 to 1547 of Henry VIII, whose Reformation effectively outlawed the established Roman Catholic faith throughout his dominions.

Matters came to an explosive head in 1641 when rebellion broke out and at least 2,000 Protestant settlers were massacred and thousands more stripped of their belongings and driven from their lands.

England had its own distractions at the time with the Civil War that culminated in the execution of Charles I in 1649, and from 1641 to 1649 Ireland was ruled by a rebel group known as the Irish Catholic Confederation, or the Confederation of Kilkenny.

One supporter of the Confederate Rebellion was Donnacha O'Callaghan, and he and his kinsfolk would pay dearly for this when a terrible vengeance was wreaked on the war-torn island in 1649 in the form of England's self-styled Lord Protector, Oliver Cromwell.

He landed at the head of a 20,000-strong army and soon held the land in a grip of iron, allowing him to implement what amounted to a policy of ethnic cleansing.

His troopers were given free rein to hunt down and kill Roman Catholic priests, while rebel estates such as those of Donnacha O'Callaghan, who was one of the reluctant signatories to the eventual Confederate surrender to Cromwell in 1652, were confiscated.

He and other leading members of the clan were 'transplanted' to Co. Clare, while the others were allowed to remain in Co. Cork as tenants of English colonists.

Those who settled in Co. Clare later established the village of O'Callaghans Mills.

An estimated 11 million acres of land were confiscated from families that had supported the rebellion, while an edict was issued stating that any native Irish found east of the River Shannon after May 1, 1654 faced either summary execution or transportation to the West Indies.

In 1690 both Donogh O'Callaghan of Mountallon, Co.Clare, and Donogh O'Callaghan of Co. Cork, were outlawed in the wake of what is known in Ireland as Cogadh an Dá Rí, or The War of the Two Kings.

Also known as the Williamite War in Ireland or the Jacobite War in Ireland, it was sparked off in 1688 when the Stuart monarch James II (James VII of Scotland) was deposed and fled into exile in France.

The Protestant William of Orange and his wife Mary were invited to take up the thrones of Scotland, Ireland, and England. James still had significant support in Ireland but his supporters were defeated and forced into surrender in September of 1691.

A peace treaty, known as the Treaty of Limerick followed, under which those willing to swear an oath of loyalty to William were allowed to remain in their native land – while those reluctant to do so were allowed to seek exile on foreign shores.

Among the latter were many Callaghans, some of who entered the military service of Spain.

One of their descendants, Don Juan O'Callaghan, a Spanish lawyer who was born in 1934, is today recognised as the O'Callaghan 'Chief of the Name', through his direct descent from the celebrated warrior Ceallachan.

Meanwhile Cornelius O'Callaghan, born in 1742, and of Shanbally Castle, at Clogheen, in Co. Clare, was later created Baron Lismore while his son became the 1st Viscount Lismore.

The parliaments of Ireland and Britain were controversially united through an Act of Union in 1800, and among the number of movements that sprang up to fight for its repeal was The Young Irelanders.

One of its leading members was John Cornelius O'Callaghan, born in 1805, and who also holds the distinction of having been one of the first Roman Catholics allowed to take up the legal profession in Ireland, following the repeal of laws that had previously barred them.

A writer on the staff of the Young Irelanders' newspaper, The Nation, O'Callaghan also became a noted historian and once famously wrote of how he 'made a daily meal of the smoked carcass of Irish history.'

Chapter four:

On the world stage

Far from the tumult of battle that the Callaghans endured for centuries, their descendants, in all the variety of spellings of the name, have gained distinction in a wide range of less violent endeavours.

In the world of politics Leonard James Callaghan, Baron Callaghan of Cardiff, was better known as the British Prime Minister and Labour Party politician **Jim Callaghan**.

Nicknamed 'Sunny Jim' or 'Big Jim', and born in Portsmouth in 1912, he served in the Royal Navy during the Second World War, reaching the rank of lieutenant.

Entering politics at the end of the war, he became Labour MP for Cardiff.

To date he is the only person to have served in what are known as all four of Britain's Great Offices of State – those of Chancellor of the Exchequer (1964-1967), Home Secretary (1967-1970), Foreign Secretary (1974-1976), and Prime Minister from 1976 until 1979.

He died in 2005 on the eve of his 93rd birthday, making him to date the longest-living British Prime Minister.

His death came only eleven days after that of his wife **Audrey, Baroness Callaghan of Cardiff**, whom he had married in 1938.

Born in 1915 in Maidstone, Kent, she was also a

politician and a tireless campaigner for children's health and welfare.

In Irish politics **Professor Kate O'Callaghan**, born in 1888, was the leading Sinn Féin politician and academic who was elected to Dáil Éireann, the Irish Parliament, in 1921. She died in 1961.

In contemporary times **Alice Callaghan**, born in 1947 in Calgary, Alberta, is the political activist, Episcopalian priest, and former Roman Catholic nun now resident in Los Angeles, where she campaigns on behalf of the city's poor and homeless.

From politics to the glamour of the silver screen, **Richard O'Callaghan** is the stage name of the actor Richard Brooke, born in London in 1940.

A son of the British actress Patricia Hayes, his many film roles include the comedies *Carry on Loving*, from 1970, and the 1971 *Carry On At Your Convenience*. He is also known for a number of stage and television roles.

Born in 1957 **Cindy O'Callaghan** is the former British actress who has now given up the stage in favour of a career as a child psychologist.

Her film roles include the 1971 Disney film *Bedknobs and Broomsticks*, the 1979 *Hanover Street* and the 1995 *I.D.* while she also appeared in the popular British television soap *EastEnders*.

Born in 1967 in Papua, New Guinea, **Jeremy Callaghan** is the Australian actor who starred in the popular television drama *Police Rescue* and who has also had roles in the *Xena: Warrior Princess*, and *Young Hercules* television series.

From Australia to Ireland **Miriam O'Callaghan**, born in 1961 in Foxrock, near Dublin, is a popular current affairs broadcaster on Radio Telefis Éireann.

In the competitive world of sport **Dr Patrick O'Callaghan** is recognised as having been one of Ireland's greatest athletes.

Born in 1905 in Derrygallow, Co. Cork, he joined the Royal Air Force medical corps in 1926 after studying medicine, returning to his native Ireland two years later.

Setting up in medical practice in Clonmel, Co. Tipperary, he also found time to pursue his passions of athletics, football, rugby, and hurling.

In 1928 he became the first person from an independent Ireland to win an Olympic medal when he took the gold in the 16lb. hammer throw event in Amsterdam.

He again took gold in the hammer at the Los Angeles Olympics four years later.

Dr O'Callaghan continued in medical practice in Clonmel until his retirement in 1984. He died seven years later.

Also in Ireland **Bill O'Callaghan**, born in Cork in 1869, was the noted hurler who played with the Redmonds Team, representing Co. Cork, in the latter two decades of the nineteenth century.

Crossing the ocean to North America, Helen Callaghan

Candaele St. Austin, born in 1923 in Vancouver, British Columbia, was better known under the name of **Helen Callaghan**.

A left-handed centre fielder, she appeared in five seasons in the All-American Girls Professional Baseball League, playing with the Minneapolis Millerettes – that later became the Fort Wayne Daises.

Inducted into the Canadian Baseball Hall of Fame, she died in 1992.

One of her five sons, Casey Candaele, has also made his name in baseball, having played for teams that include the Montreal Expos, Houston Astros, and Cleveland Indians.

In ice hockey **Ryan Callaghan**, born in 1985 in Rochester, New York is, at the time of writing, a right-winger with the New York Rangers, while on the cricket pitch **David Callaghan**, born in 1965, is the former South African cricketer who played 29 times for his country.

On the field of European football the player who, at the time of writing, holds the record for the most appearances for the top English club Liverpool is **Ian Callaghan**, born in the city in 1942.

Making his debut with the club in 1960, the right-winger went on to play for the team for no less than 856 times, scoring 69 goals, before leaving in 1978. He played for a time with the U.S. team Fort Lauderdale; awarded an M.B.E. in 1974, he also won four caps for England.

On the rugby pitch **Donncha O'Callaghan**, born in 1979, is the Irish Rugby Union lock forward who was a member of the Munster team that won the 2006 Heineken European Cup.

In the creative world of literature **Edward Morley Callaghan** was the Canadian short story writer, novelist, playwright, and radio and television personality who was born in Toronto in 1903.

He turned to journalism after studying law, working for a time during the 1920s at the *Toronto Star* beside fellow journalist and then budding writer Ernest Hemingway, formerly of the *Kansas City Star*.

In his 1963 memoir *That Summer in Paris*, Callaghan recalled how his friend Hemingway had challenged him to a boxing match while they were living in Paris.

Callaghan accepted the challenge and knocked Hemingway to the floor.

Awarded the Royal Society of Canada's Lorne Pierce Medal in 1960 and made a Companion of the Order of Canada in 1982, his many books include the 1928 *Strange Fugitive*, *The Loved and the Lost* (1951), *A Fine and Private Peace* and *A Wild Old Man on the Road*, published two years before his death in 1990.

His son **Barry Callaghan**, born in Toronto in 1937, is the author, poet, and anthologist whose works include *The Hogg Poems and Drawings* and the 2007 *Between Trains*.

Born in Newry in 1968, **Conor O'Callaghan** is the Irish poet whose published collections include the 1993 *The History of Rain*, while **Edmund O'Callaghan**, born in 1797 in Mallow, Co. Cork, was the medical doctor and journalist who became involved with the early nineteenth century political reform movement in Lower Canada.

Elected to the Legislative Assembly of Lower Canada in 1834, he fled to the United States three years later after a warrant was issued for his arrest in connection with the Lower Canada Rebellion.

He later became secretary-archivist of the State of New York.

Born in Dublin in 1944, **Mary Callaghan** is the writer and biographer whose works include the 1989 *Kitty O'Shea: A Life of Kathleen Parnell*.

On the high seas **Daniel J. Callaghan**, born in 1890 in San Francisco, was the Rear Admiral in the United States Navy who was posthumously awarded the Congressional Medal of Honor for his valour during the battle of Guadalcanal in November 1942.

Two U.S. Navy ships have been named in his honour.

Also known by the name of Marlene Wallace, **Marlene Callaghan** is the American actress and photographer born in 1937 in Ventura, California.

A former Playboy model, her renowned portrait photographs include subjects ranging from Anthony Quinn and Hugh Hefner to former U.S. President Jimmy Carter.

Also behind the camera lens **Harry Callahan**, born in Detroit in 1912 and who died in 1999, was the highly innovative American photographer whose work included experimentation with multiple exposures.

In the art world **Kenneth Callahan**, born in 1905 in Spokane, Washington, and who died in 1986, was the Abstract Expressionist painter and critic who was a founder of what is known as America's Northwest School.

He was also curator for a time of the Seattle Art Museum.

In the world of medicine **John Callaghan**, born in 1923 in Hamilton, Ontario, and who died in 2004, was the pioneer of open-heart surgery in Alberta.

Made an Officer of the Order of Canada in 1985, he was inducted a year later into the Alberta Order of Excellence.

Callaghans have also been at the forefront of pioneering scientific research – and no less so that **Professor Paul Callaghan**, the prominent physicist and author who was born in 1947 in Wanganui, New Zealand and who was made a Principal Companion of the New Zealand Order of Merit in 2007.

Key dates in Ireland's history from the first settlers to the formation of the Irish Republic:

circa 7000 B.C.	Arrival and settlement of Stone Age people.
circa 3000 B.C.	Arrival of settlers of New Stone Age period.
circa 600 B.C.	First arrival of the Celts.
200 A.D.	Establishment of Hill of Tara, Co. Meath, as seat of the High Kings.
circa 432 A.D.	Christian mission of St. Patrick.
800-920 A.D.	Invasion and subsequent settlement of Vikings.
1002 A.D.	Brian Boru recognised as High King.
1014	Brian Boru killed at battle of Clontarf.
1169-1170	Cambro-Norman invasion of the island.
1171	Henry II claims Ireland for the English Crown.
1366	Statutes of Kilkenny ban marriage between native Irish and English.
1529-1536	England's Henry VIII embarks on religious Reformation.
1536	Earl of Kildare rebels against the Crown.
1541	Henry VIII declared King of Ireland.
1558	Accession to English throne of Elizabeth I.
1565	Battle of Affane.
1569-1573	First Desmond Rebellion.
1579-1583	Second Desmond Rebellion.
1594-1603	Nine Years War.
1606	Plantation' of Scottish and English settlers.
1607	Flight of the Earls.
1632-1636	Annals of the Four Masters compiled.
1641	Rebellion over policy of plantation and other grievances.
1649	Beginning of Cromwellian conquest.
1688	Flight into exile in France of Catholic Stuart monarch James II as Protestant Prince William of Orange invited to take throne of England along with his wife, Mary.
1689	William and Mary enthroned as joint monarchs; siege of Derry.
1690	Jacobite forces of James defeated by William at battle of the Boyne (July) and Dublin taken.

1691	Athlone taken by William; Jacobite defeats follow at Aughrim, Galway, and Limerick; conflict ends with Treaty of Limerick (October) and Irish officers allowed to leave for France.
1695	Penal laws introduced to restrict rights of Catholics; banishment of Catholic clergy.
1704	Laws introduced constricting rights of Catholics in landholding and public office.
1728	Franchise removed from Catholics.
1791	Foundation of United Irishmen republican movement.
1796	French invasion force lands in Bantry Bay.
1798	Defeat of Rising in Wexford and death of United Irishmen leaders Wolfe Tone and Lord Edward Fitzgerald.
1800	Act of Union between England and Ireland.
1803	Dublin Rising under Robert Emmet.
1829	Catholics allowed to sit in Parliament.
1845-1849	The Great Hunger: thousands starve to death as potato crop fails and thousands more emigrate.
1856	Phoenix Society founded.
1858	Irish Republican Brotherhood established.
1873	Foundation of Home Rule League.
1893	Foundation of Gaelic League.
1904	Foundation of Irish Reform Association.
1913	Dublin strikes and lockout.
1916	Easter Rising in Dublin and proclamation of an Irish Republic.
1917	Irish Parliament formed after Sinn Fein election victory.
1919-1921	War between Irish Republican Army and British Army.
1922	Irish Free State founded, while six northern counties remain part of United Kingdom as Northern Ireland, or Ulster; civil war up until 1923 between rival republican groups.
1949	Foundation of Irish Republic after all remaining constitutional links with Britain are severed.